Scripture Up

affirmation journal

Also by Dennis Schleicher

Is He Nuts?
Why a Gay Man Would Become
a Member of the Church of Jesus Christ

Scripture Up

affirmation journal

Strengthening *God's* Message

Old Testament &
Pearl of Great Price

Dennis Schleicher

CFI
An imprint of Cedar Fort, Inc.
Springville, Utah

I dedicate this journal to my dear friend, Sister Maggie Slighte.
Without her continued encouragement and motivating me
to complete this project, this would not exist.

I also dedicate this to the thousands of followers and friends on
Instagram and other social media platforms who have provided countless
encouragement and strength to make this project a reality with all of
your comments and messages. I consider all of you family.

© 2021 Dennis Schleicher
All rights reserved.

No part of this book may be reproduced in any form whatsoever, whether by graphic, visual, electronic, film, microfilm, tape recording, or any other means, without prior written permission of the publisher, except in the case of brief passages embodied in critical reviews and articles.

This is not an official publication of The Church of Jesus Christ of Latter-day Saints. The opinions and views expressed herein belong solely to the author and do not necessarily represent the opinions or views of Cedar Fort, Inc. Permission for the use of sources, graphics, and photos is also solely the responsibility of the author.

ISBN 13: 978-1-4621-4159-3

Published by CFI, an imprint of Cedar Fort, Inc.
2373 W. 700 S., Springville, UT 84663
Distributed by Cedar Fort, Inc., www.cedarfort.com

Library of Congress Control Number: 2021939917

Cover and text design by Courtney Proby
Cover design © 2021 Cedar Fort, Inc.

Printed in the United States of America

10 9 8 7 6 5 4 3 2 1

Printed on acid-free paper

Contents

From Fear to Love in Five Positive Steps:
Hope, Healing, Courage, Strength, and Love 1

Fear. 4

Hope. 38

Healing. 72

Courage 106

Strength 140

Love 174

Recommended Reading 208

About the Author 209

From Fear to Love in Five Positive Steps

Fear is the root of all challenges and the foundation for most faith crises. How do we overcome fear? With the help of God and His Son, Jesus Christ. They can bless us with

Hope, which leads to *healing*.

Healing, which lays the groundwork for *courage*.

Courage, which gives us *strength*.

Strength, which motivates us to keep trying, and

Love, the love of God, self, and others—which brings us self-acceptance and the knowledge that we are enough in our Heavenly Father's eyes.

Instead of allowing fear to control you and prevent you from having what you really want from life, use it to fuel your goals and dreams. Let God help you overcome fear. Allow Him into your life—you will never regret it.

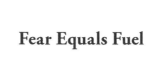

Fear Equals Fuel

It's a common belief that once a testimony is gained, it's smooth sailing from then on. However, gaining a testimony is not a one-time discovery. It's a lifelong commitment that keeps you reaching for your purpose. It's a long road of developmental trial and error. Studying the scriptures is a necessary habit that we must develop in order to keep our testimony alive. We cannot gain exaltation without it!

Of course it's difficult at times to keep trying, to keep living the gospel and studying the scriptures, especially when life is hard, but men are that they might have joy, so enjoy this life. You are enough in His eyes! Stop comparing your past or behind-the-scenes mistakes to your future, your self-esteem, and your self-worth. The Atonement of Jesus Christ is the power that gives us the ability—our agency—to renew our covenants and constantly strengthen our relationship with Him.

Why Do I Use Scripture Affirmations?

I don't believe in the word *should*. For many years I would say, "I *should* read more scripture," "I *should* eat healthier," "I *should* start exercising more . . ." And then I learned that when I replaced the word *should* with *will* or *can*, such as "I *will* read more scripture," "I *can* eat healthier," "I *can* and *will* exercise more," I actually followed through on it. It's empowering to use words of action.

When you use the power of positive action words to fuel your life's purpose, you will notice that your subconscious mind will naturally lean toward developing more healthy habits, and the more good habits you develop, the closer you become to being who you really want to be.

How Do Affirmations Work?

Affirmations are a time-honored method of improving your core beliefs. They are a simple tool that can literally turn around your habitual negative thoughts. Affirmations can assist you with self-regulation, self-worth, self-awareness, and self-confidence.

Repeating positive phrases to yourself can help you move through tricky situations. One such phrase that can be of assistance in many situations is, "I can do this!"

Once using affirmations becomes a habit, they will come to mind when a healthy belief is challenged.

If your affirmation is, "I am wonderful just the way I am" and you are told you are stupid, the affirmation can be recalled to remind you of what you really are. Instead, you'll think, "I'm not stupid! I'm wonderful!"

Without positive reinforcement, you might believe the lie you just heard and take that lie upon yourself.

The more an affirmation is repeated, positive or negative, the stronger it becomes.

It is important that we learn to take control of our belief systems. The younger we learn, the easier it is. Negative beliefs can impact our lives greatly and can be difficult to change as we grow older.

Why Scripture Affirmations?

Affirmations are more effective when repeated, and it's best to repeat an affirmation three times, saying the words louder and with more confidence each time. The repetition helps affirm the belief.

You might want to work on one affirmation a day, or one a week, depending on how confident you feel with each affirmation. If you seem to struggle with an affirmation, you might want to continue working on that one longer. Incorporating scripture will reinforce your affirmations.

I can testify that gospel-centered affirmations and study have strengthened my testimony.

I do know that God loves me and I am His son whom He accepts without reservation. My faith in this one thing is what lifts me above the emotional storm clouds and helps me to soar through life. I have confidence.

—Dennis Schleicher

Always choose to remember Him.

Fear thou not; for I [am] with thee: be not
dismayed; for I [am] thy God: I will strengthen
thee; yea, I will help thee; yea, I will uphold thee
with the right hand of my righteousness.

Isaiah 41:10

How do I think or feel when I read this?

All is well with my own connection to the Holy Ghost.

The Kingdom of heaven is like a merchant on the lookout for choice pearls. When he discovered a pearl of great value, he sold everything he owned and bought it!

Matthew 13:45–46

How do I think or feel when I read this?

_____

_____

_____

_____

_____

_____

_____

_____

_____

_____

I feel God's infinite love always.

We believe in God, the Eternal Father, and in His Son, Jesus Christ, and in the Holy Ghost.

Article of Faith 1:1

How do I think or feel when I read this?

_____

_____

_____

_____

_____

_____

_____

_____

_____

_____

_____

_____

Having faith brings me comfort.

I sought the LORD, and he heard me,
and delivered me from all my fears.

Psalms 34:4

How do I think or feel when I read this?

I trust in the Lord and am safe.

The fear of man bringeth a snare: but whoso putteth his trust in the LORD shall be safe.

Proverbs 29:25

I am always prayerfully expressing my gratitude.

We believe that men will be punished for their own sins, and not for Adam's transgression.

Articles of Faith 1:2

How do I think or feel when I read this?

_____

_____

_____

_____

_____

_____

_____

_____

_____

_____

Faith strengthens my trust.

What time I am afraid, I will trust in thee.

Psalms 56:3–4

How do I think or feel when I read this?

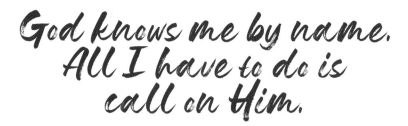

God knows me by name. All I have to do is call on Him.

Heal me, O LORD, and I shall be healed; save me, and I shall be saved: for thou [art] my praise.

Jeremiah 17:14

How do I think or feel when I read this?

_____

_____

_____

_____

_____

_____

_____

_____

_____

_____

Reflect and Respond to Fear

What have I learned about fear through my scripture study?

Answers to prayer and affirmations: _____

_____

_____

_____

_____

_____

_____

_____

Messages you received concerning the consequences of fear

1. _____

2. _____

3. _____

"Hesitation and doubt are legitimate feelings to have, but what you do next is the challenge."

—Dennis Schleicher

I follow the covenant path constantly; therefore, I feel and see His blessings.

Blessed [is] the man that trusteth in the LORD, and whose hope the LORD is.

Jeremiah 17:7

How do I think or feel when I read this?

I will ask God and the Holy Ghost for answers.

We believe that the first principles and ordinances of the Gospel are: first, Faith in the Lord Jesus Christ; second, Repentance; third, Baptism by immersion for the remission of sins; fourth, Laying on of hands for the gift of the Holy Ghost.

Articles of Faith 1:4

How do I think or feel when I read this?

My vision is clear; I know all things are possible through faith.

My soul, wait in silence for God
only, for my hope is from Him.

Psalm 62:5

How do I think or feel when I read this?

_____

_____

_____

_____

_____

_____

_____

_____

_____

_____

I have a direct connection to Heavenly Father.

We believe that a man must be called of God, by prophecy, and by the laying on of hands by those who are in authority, to preach the Gospel and administer in the ordinances thereof.

Articles of Faith 1:5

How do I think or feel when I read this?

God does not want me to struggle. He is here for me.

Be strong and of a good courage, fear not, nor be afraid of them: for the LORD thy God, he [it is] that doth go with thee; he will not fail thee, nor forsake thee.

Deuteronomy 31:6

How do I think or feel when I read this?

54

I turn fear into fuel.
God always has my back.

Fear thou not; for I [am] with thee: be not dismayed; for I [am]
thy God: I will strengthen thee; yea, I will help thee; yea, I will
uphold thee with the right hand of my righteousness.

Isaiah 41:10

How do I think or feel when I read this?

_____

_____

_____

_____

_____

_____

_____

_____

_____

God will move mountains, if I let Him.

And now, Lord, what wait I for? my hope [is] in thee.

Psalms 39:7

How do I think or feel when I read this?

I have strength knowing all things are possible through God.

We believe in the same organization that existed in the Primitive Church, namely, apostles, prophets, pastors, teachers, evangelists, and so forth.

Articles of Faith 1:6

How do I think or feel when I read this?

_____

_____

_____

_____

_____

_____

_____

_____

_____

_____

_____

Reflect and Respond to Hope

What have I learned about hope through my scripture study?

Answers to prayer and affirmations: _____

_____

_____

_____

_____

_____

_____

_____

Messages you received about the blessing of hope

1. _____

2. _____

3. _____

"By listening instead of lecturing, you can gain knowledge and understanding, which will help you love them more."

—Dennis Schleicher

If I can take time to do something for myself today, then I can help others.

Fear thou not; for I [am] with thee: be not dismayed; for I [am] thy God: I will strengthen thee; yea, I will help thee; yea, I will uphold thee with the right hand of my righteousness.

Isaiah 41:10

How do I think or feel when I read this?

I am healing myself every moment; therefore, I am helping to heal others.

Behold, I will bring it health and cure, and I will cure them, and will reveal unto them the abundance of peace and truth.

Jeremiah 33:6

How do I think or feel when I read this?

_____

_____

_____

_____

_____

_____

_____

_____

_____

_____

I humbly give all my burdens to God.

But he [was] wounded for our transgressions, [he was] bruised for our iniquities: the chastisement of our peace [was] upon him; and with his stripes we are healed.

Isaiah 53:5

How do I think or feel when I read this?

_____

_____

_____

_____

_____

_____

_____

_____

_____

_____

I pray humbly to our Savior, Jesus Christ, asking Him for what I need to know now.

We believe in the gift of tongues, prophecy, revelation, visions, healing, interpretation of tongues, and so forth.

Articles of Faith 1:7

How do I think or feel when I read this?

Right now I will call and ask for someone to pray for me. It's going to be okay.

We believe all that God has revealed, all that He does now reveal, and we believe that He will yet reveal many great and important things pertaining to the Kingdom of God.

Articles of Faith 1:9

How do I think or feel when I read this?

_____

_____

_____

_____

_____

_____

_____

_____

_____

_____

_____

I will kneel in prayer, asking Heavenly Father for health, love, strength, and a testimony.

We believe in the literal gathering of Israel and in the restoration of the Ten Tribes; that Zion (the New Jerusalem) will be built upon the American continent; that Christ will reign personally upon the earth; and, that the earth will be renewed and receive its paradisiacal glory.

Articles of Faith 1:10

How do I think or feel when I read this?

How can I help someone who is struggling? How can I help myself?

He healeth the broken in heart,
and bindeth up their wounds.

Psalms 147:3

How do I think or feel when I read this?

I call upon God daily to help me with...

Heal me, O Lord, and I will be healed; save me
and I will be saved, for you are the one I praise.

Jeremiah 17:14

How do I think or feel when I read this?

Reflect and Respond to Healing

What have I learned about healing through my scripture study?

Answers to prayer and affirmations: _____

_____

_____

_____

_____

_____

_____

_____

Messages you received concerning the miracle of being healed

1. _____

2. _____

3. _____

"Be more like Christ. Listen to others. Let's turn up the love, lead by example, and most important, just be yourself.

—Dennis Schleicher

My strength in God is constantly growing by ...

We believe the Bible to be the word of God
as far as it is translated correctly; we also believe the
Book of Mormon to be the word of God.

Articles of Faith 1:8

How do I think or feel when I read this?

_____

_____

_____

_____

_____

_____

_____

_____

_____

_____

Through strength, I have unlimited courage to endure to the end.

Be strong and of a good courage, fear not, nor be afraid of them: for the LORD thy God, he [it is] that doth go with thee; he will not fail thee, nor forsake thee.

Deuteronomy 31:6

How do I think or feel when I read this?

I find comfort and courage in helping myself; therefore I can help others.

Fear thou not; for I [am] with thee: be not dismayed; for I [am] thy God: I will strengthen thee; yea, I will help thee; yea, I will uphold thee with the right hand of my righteousness.

Isaiah 41:10

How do I think or feel when I read this?

God will protect me from all evils. He will fight for me as long as I am a faithful servant.

For the LORD your God [is] he that goeth with you, to fight for you against your enemies, to save you.

Deuteronomy 20:4

How do I think or feel when I read this?

_____

_____

_____

_____

_____

_____

_____

_____

_____

_____

My courage is strengthening, and I am able to trust in the power of Christ.

We claim the privilege of worshiping Almighty God according to the dictates of our own conscience, and allow all men the same privilege, let them worship how, where, or what they may.

Articles of Faith 1:11

How do I think or feel when I read this?

My courage gives me strength to soar above the emotional clouds. I have confidence.

But they that wait upon the LORD shall renew [their] strength; they shall mount up with wings as eagles; they shall run, and not be weary; [and] they shall walk, and not faint.

Isaiah 40:31

How do I think or feel when I read this?

My hope in God is endless; my courage is strong.

Be of good courage, and he shall strengthen your heart, all ye that hope in the LORD.

Psalms 31:24

How do I think or feel when I read this?

My courage in this one thing gives me the strength I need.

The LORD [is] my strength and song, and he is become my salvation: he [is] my God, and I will prepare him an habitation; my father's God, and I will exalt him.

Exodus 15:2

How do I think or feel when I read this?

Reflect and Respond to Courage

What have I learned about courage through my scripture study?

Answers to prayer and affirmations: _____

_____

_____

_____

_____

_____

_____

_____

Messages you received about the benefits of having courage

1. _____

2. _____

3. _____

"We are all unique children of God on our own individualized journeys. Don't ever let another person's opinion of you define your self-worth. What anyone else thinks is irrelevant. The Lord's opinion is the one that matters, and He thinks the world of you."

—Dennis Schleicher

God has given me the spirit of power, love, and a sound mind.

Though thy beginning was small yet thy latter end should greatly increase.

Job 8:7

How do I think or feel when I read this?

I am strong and secure.

Be of good courage, and he shall strengthen
your heart, all ye that hope in the Lord.

Job 8:7

_____

_____

_____

_____

_____

_____

_____

_____

_____

_____

My strength lifts me up to God. He will never let me down. He will keep me soaring above.

We believe in being subject to kings, presidents, rulers, and magistrates, in obeying, honoring, and sustaining the law.

Articles of Faith 1:12

How do I think or feel when I read this?

_____

_____

_____

_____

_____

_____

_____

_____

_____

_____

_____

Because of God's mighty presence, I am strong and secure.

And I, God, said: Let there be light; and there was light.

Moses 2:3

How do I think or feel when I read this?

_____

_____

_____

_____

_____

_____

_____

_____

Knowing how strong Christ is, any weakness I might have, I choose to turn into strength.

We believe in being honest, true, chaste, benevolent, virtuous, and in doing good to all men; indeed, we may say that we follow the admonition of Paul—We believe all things, we hope all things, we have endured many things, and hope to be able to endure all things. If there is anything virtuous, lovely, or of good report or praiseworthy, we seek after these things.

Articles of Faith 1:13

How do I think or feel when I read this?

I am not afraid to call upon Him, asking for strength when I need His hand.

I would seek unto God and unto God would I commit my cause.

Job 5:8

How do I think or feel when I read this?

_____

_____

_____

_____

_____

_____

_____

_____

_____

_____

My joy for God is mighty. My strength for Him provides me peace and comfort.

For in those days there shall also arise false Christs, and false prophets, and shall show great signs and wonders, insomuch, that, if possible, they shall deceive the very elect, who are the elect according to the covenant.

Joseph Smith—Matthew 1

How do I think or feel when I read this?

Even during the darkest hour, my increasing strength is strong.

He giveth power to the faint; and to [them that have] no might he increaseth strength.

Isaiah 40:29–31

How do I think or feel when I read this?

Reflect and Respond to Strength

What have I learned about strength through my scripture study?

Answers to prayer and affirmations: _____

_____

_____

_____

_____

_____

_____

Messages you received about having spiritual strength

1. _____

2. _____

3. _____

"I do know that God loves me and I am His son whom He accepts without reservation. My faith in this one thing is what lifts me above the emotional storm clouds and helps me soar through life. I have confidence."

—Dennis Schleicher

Charity is the foundation of service and love for others.

After all that has been said, the greatest and most important duty is to preach the Gospel.

History of the Church, 2:478

How do I think or feel when I read this?

_____

_____

_____

_____

_____

_____

_____

_____

_____

_____

_____

I am constantly loving myself; therefore I can love others.

A friend loveth at all times, and a brother is born for adversity.

Proverbs 17:17

How do I think or feel when I read this?

_____

_____

_____

_____

_____

_____

_____

_____

_____

_____

I will love my neighbor as I would want to be loved.

Hatred stirreth up strifes: but love covereth all sins.

Proverbs 10:12

How do I think or feel when I read this?

Through the Atonement of Christ, I constantly feel His presence and love.

Cause me to hear thy loving kindness in the morning;
for in thee do I trust: cause me to know the way wherein
I should walk; for I lift up my soul unto thee.

Psalm 143:8

How do I think or feel when I read this?

_____

_____

_____

_____

_____

_____

_____

_____

_____

_____

_____

Because of my faith in Christ, I will have eternal Life.

Lord, I have loved the habitation of thy house,
and the place where thine honour dwelleth.

Psalm 26:8

How do I think or feel when I read this?

My love for and relationship with God is personal. I am constantly growing stronger as I ask Him for knowledge and wisdom.

And unto thy brethren have I said, and also given commandment, that they should love one another, and that they should choose me, their Father; but behold, they are without affection, and they hate their own blood.

Pearl of Great Price, Moses 7:33

How do I think or feel when I read this?

I am perfectly content with my relationship with God.

Then Jonathan and David made a covenant,
because he loved him as his own soul.

Samuel 18:3

How do I think or feel when I read this?

Today I am being charitable to myself by pondering scripture. Therefore, tomorrow I can be charitable to others.

The Lord hath appeared of old unto me, saying,
Yea, I have loved thee with an everlasting love:
therefore with lovingkindness have I drawn thee.

Jeremiah 31:3

How do I think or feel when I read this?

_____

_____

_____

_____

_____

_____

_____

_____

_____

Reflect and Respond to Love

What have I learned about love through my scripture study?

Answers to prayer and affirmations: _____

_____

_____

_____

_____

_____

_____

_____

What I have learned about the precious gift of love

1. _____

2. _____

3. _____

Hesitation and doubt are legitimate feelings to have, but what you do next is the challenge. I've learned that the best response is, What do I need to learn from this? All of this is happening for a reason to help me become a stronger person inside and out.

—Dennis Schleicher

Recommended Books

More than the Tattooed Mormon, Second Edition
Al Carraway

Wildly Optimistic, Gaining New Perspective for Life's Challenges
Al Carraway

Love Boldly: Embracing Your LGBTQ Loved Ones and Your Faith
Becky Mackintosh

My Dad's a Muslim, My Mom's a Lesbian, and I'm a Latter-day Saint
Mike Ramsey

Listen, Learn, and Love : Embracing LGBTQ Latter-day Saints
Richard Ostler

Without the Mask: Coming Out and Coming Into God's Light
Charlie Bird

Stand Guard at the Door of Your Mind
Drew Young

About the Author

Dennis Schleicher is a public speaker within the Church and has traveled worldwide, speaking and inspiring others with his conversion story and faith during difficult times. A writer, lifestyle reporter, and motivational speaker, Dennis is president and publicity director of the Connecticut Authors & Publishers Association.

Dennis currently works as a literary agent representing Christian authors. He has worked at several Fortune 500 companies, including working as a regional sales manager representing a multimillion-dollar territory within the professional beauty industry. It is through Dennis's work experience that he learned to effectively communicate with others and achieve his future goals.

At age seventeen, he appeared on seven talk shows, including *Larry King Live* and *Sally Jessy Raphael*, after being a victim of a brutal hate crime that occurred in his high school.

Dennis now serves as ward elder's quorum first counselor and ward mission leader. He also assists mission presidents, leaders, sisters, and elders throughout the world to better understand how to serve and help the LGBTQ+ community, creating a better understanding among all people.